∞

Making Christ's Peace
a Part of Your Life

Other books by Dietrich von Hildebrand
available from Sophia Institute Press

Confidence in God
The New Tower of Babel
Marriage: The Mystery of Faithful Love
Love, Marriage, and the Catholic Conscience
Humility: Wellspring of Virtue
Transformation in Christ

Dietrich von Hildebrand

Making
Christ's Peace
A Part of Your Life

SOPHIA INSTITUTE PRESS®
Manchester, New Hampshire

Sophia Institute Press®
Box 5284, Manchester, NH 03108
1-800-888-9344
www.sophiainstitute.com

Library of Congress Cataloging-in-Publication Data

Von Hildebrand, Dietrich, 1889-
    Making Christ's peace a part of your life / Dietrich von
    Hildebrand.
        p.   cm.
    Includes bibliographical references.
    ISBN 0-918477-80-8 (pbk. : alk. paper)
    1. Peace — Religious aspects — Catholic Church.
        2. Christian life — Catholic authors. 3. Peace of
    mind — Religious aspects — Catholic Church.
    I. Title.
BX1795.P43V66 1998
241'.4 — DC21   98-34832   CIP

98 99 00 01 10 9 8 7 6 5 4 3 2 1

∞

Contents

∞

*Making Christ's Peace
a Part of Your Life*

∞

Peace Begins Within Us

∞

Peace is a basic word of the Gospel; it occupies a central place in Christian Revelation. Indeed, it is the primal word addressed to mankind by the message of the New Covenant: "Glory to God in the highest: and on earth peace to men of good will."[1] Again, in His parting speech to the disciples, our Lord says: "Peace I leave with you: my peace I give unto you."[2]

The object of the Christians' Advent longing was, above all, the Messiah, the bringer of peace, who would heal the strife of the world; the strife that, more tangibly than anything else, expresses the disharmony of a fallen creation. A touching desire and hope for peace cries out in the vision of Isaiah the prophet: "The wolf shall dwell with the lamb; and the leopard shall lie down with the kid. The calf and the lion and the sheep shall abide together; and a little child shall lead them."[3] And

[1] 1 Luke 2:14.
[2] John 14:27.
[3] Isa. 11:6.

the psalmist sings: "Justice and peace have kissed."[4] At Christmas, the Church hails the Savior as *Princeps Pacis*, Prince of Peace. In the Mass, the faithful before receiving Holy Communion exchange the sign of peace as a sign that all discord among them has been obliterated. On Holy Thursday, in the Liturgy of the Washing of the Feet, the Church sings: "Let malicious upbraidings cease; let wranglings cease. And may Christ, our God, be in the midst of us." *Pax* ("peace") is the motto of the Benedictines; *pax et bonum* ("peace and good"), that of the Franciscans.

∞

Peace is a central theme of Christian Revelation

No one who does not love peace as a high good, and whose heart is not scorched with pain at the sight of strife or by the thought of disharmony, has ever really understood the Gospels or can ever truly love Christ. Our imitation of Christ — and the more so, our transformation in Christ — necessarily involves a love for peace, a concord of hearts, a horror of all forms of discord, disunion, and dissension.

[4] Ps. 84:11 (RSV = Ps. 85:10).

Nothing evokes more constant blame from St. Paul in his epistles than the dissension and conflict arising in the Christian communities. Again and again he urgently admonishes the faithful to keep peace among one another: "I beg of Evodia and I beseech Syntyche to be of one mind in the Lord."[5] It is a specific stigma of abysmal separation from God to maintain a quarrelsome and cantankerous attitude, a morbid delight in bickerings and conflicts, a perverse pleasure derived from disharmony.

However, an essential love for peace and aversion to strife is not enough. It does not by itself vouch for our being actually able to behave as peacemakers and to overcome the temptations of enmity in the evolving situations of life. The immanent logic of various events and relationships, with their autonomous demands and the interests implied in them, are only too apt to entangle in discords and conflicts even such men who essentially love and seek peace.

To begin with, we must make a fundamental distinction. The dangers to peace arising from a multiplicity of social contacts and oppositions require a different treatment, according as they originate in a situation whose

[5] Phil. 4:2.

7

theme is supplied by our interests as such (even though taken in a wide sense) or in a situation in which we are striving for some high objective value — in the extreme case, the kingdom of God itself. Let us next consider the first type of situation.

∞

We must judge objectively when we feel wronged

There is a kind of people who, although by nature peace-loving and far from quarrelsome, are so touchy as to feel insulted and wronged on the slightest provocation. The sense of being injured will incite them to acute outbreaks of anger or to more latent reactions of ill temper and sulking, and thus involve them in clashes and disagreements.

Against this susceptibility, which is wholly incompatible with a life conceived in the spirit of Christ, we must wage a relentless fight. Whenever we feel offended, we should at once examine before God whether we are not really only indulging our susceptibility, without having suffered any objective wrong at all.

Perhaps the "offender" has done no worse than tell a truth which irritates us because it is unpalatable to our pride. Or again, it may be our jealousy that makes us fretful. Our egocentric squeamishness, too, may often present other people's actions or utterances in a false and distorting light. Sometimes, again, it is our distrusting disposition that incites us to look for a sting of insult or an edge of malevolence in whatever people say. It may also happen that a stranger's words unintentionally strike upon a sore spot in our emotional system, an inferiority complex for instance. We then feel offended and unjustly put him down as tactless.

In view of these numerous possibilities of error, it is a Christian's duty always to examine, with a wholesome mistrust of himself, the objective side of the question when he feels wronged or insulted. Confronting his feelings and their occasion with God, he must attain to a freedom of mind enabling him to ascertain, with his vision unblurred by any subjective biases, whether he has suffered any wrong in the objective sense of the term. If this proves not to be the case, he must wholly and thoroughly dissolve his rancor — have it "shattered upon Christ," as the Rule of St. Benedict puts it — and approach the misjudged "offender" with particular friendliness.

A great many people shirk this duty because, in their general reliance upon their nature, they implicitly trust its reactions and unquestioningly interpret their moods as the index of an objective fact. They deem their subjective state of mind the more sensitive instrument, whose findings cannot be tested and corrected by the clumsier methods of intellectual analysis.

This overvaluation of one's subjective impressions is a tremendous mistake; for in truth, their legitimate role is not to outrun or supersede objective thinking but merely to provide it with initial stimuli and with part of its materials.

∞

We must forgive all objective wrongs we suffer

If, on the other hand, an objective wrong has been inflicted upon us, we must endeavor truly to forgive it. To be sure, the experiences we have had with a person (inasmuch as they disclose to us the general defects of his character, apart from our personal interests on which they have happened to impinge) may warrant on our part the drawing of certain consequences.

We may decide no longer to trust him. But we must not let a state of conflict establish itself. In our encounter with Christ and remembering His words, "Love your enemies; do good to them that hate you; and pray for them that persecute and calumniate you,"[6] as well as the many wrongs we have ourselves perpetrated upon others, we must truly and honestly dissolve rancor, all embitterment, all enmity. We must definitively expunge the debt our offender has contracted toward us. We should face him in serene charity, without any sullenness or cramped self-consciousness. The negative consequences we cannot help drawing in his regard must, without any trace of irritation and asperity, exclusively imply a noble and serene sorrow.

∞

Ignoring objective evils does not establish true peace

Moreover, the attitude of rancorous enmity is not the only antithesis to the Christian spirit of forgiveness. Another attitude opposed to it is that of simply ignoring the wrong inflicted upon us, as though nothing had happened. This aberration may result from laziness, from faintness of heart, or from a sickly, mawkish clinging to outward peace. We hold our comfort too dear to fight it out with our aggressor; or again, we feel terrified at the thought of any tension or hostility, and fear lest a sharp

[6] Matt. 5:44.

reaction on our part should exasperate the adversary; or perhaps we yield just out of respect for the abstract idol of peace.

This is a kind of behavior far remote from the genuine love of peace or from a genuine spirit of forgiveness. It can never achieve the true harmony of peace, but at best a superficial cloaking of enmity, a mood of false joviality which drags our souls toward the peripheral.

Also, people who behave thus fail to consider the moral damage that their supineness is likely to inflict on others. It is very often necessary to draw a person's attention to the wrong he has done us — in fact, necessary for his own good. To pass over it in silence may easily encourage him in his bad dispositions.

But we cannot reproach him to good purpose — that is, without provoking strife — unless we have ourselves attained to that serene attitude cleansed of all impulsive resentment; in other words, unless we have truly forgiven him. When we have risen above the narrow logic of the situation and ceased to face our fellow man as an antagonist with whom we are locked in strife on a battleground; when we have acquired in Christ that holy freedom, that humility before God and the human soul — His image — which confers upon us a sovereign detachment from the immanency of the situation, then only shall we be able to correct our offender in a manner really conducive to his good. Again, when we have risen above the mood of regarding his awareness or admission of his wrong as a satisfaction to ourselves, then only shall we be able to ponder judiciously and to decide pertinently whether or not it is necessary for us to remonstrate with him for his good.

∞

Peace between friends requires that
wrongs be confronted and forgiven

All this refers to our disagreements with comparative strangers, persons with whom we are not linked by close bonds of friendship or love. Where such bonds do exist, the case is essentially different. Here it is strictly required by the nature of the relationship that our partner shall recognize and regret the wrong he has done to us. Here we must not quit the common level on which we are joined with him, for by so doing, we should act against the spirit of the relation that unites us and, indeed, implicitly disavow our friendship. In this case, the other person has a legitimate claim to the continuance of our being partners.

Making Christ's Peace a Part of Your Life

Most certainly we must forgive him, too; but here we must desire that he recognize and repent of his wrong, not merely for his own good, but for the sake of our relationship itself — of the restoration of that intimate union of hearts which essentially demands the clearing up of all misunderstandings and the healing of all disharmonies. For that union of hearts is an objective good which we must guard and cultivate, and which imposes certain obligations on us.

True, here as in other cases we must not let the autonomous mechanism of the situation run away with us and must carefully refrain from repaying an injury in kind. As victims of an aggression here and now, we must — under these specific conditions, too — detach ourselves from the situation of the moment and answer all gestures of irritation, all moral blows, with kindness and charity only.

Yet, here we can on no account content ourselves with an act of inward forgiveness: at the proper moment, we must in love draw our friend's attention to his wrong and maintain our desire for his redressing it. However, we cannot do this in the right way before we have truly forgiven him, before all bitterness and irritation on our part have yielded to a purified, unselfish pain.

Peace Begins Within Us

Our admonition should not bear, properly speaking, the note of a reproach. It should rather be in the character of a humble and amicable exposition of our grief, a gentle invitation to our friend to consider the matter in a valid perspective and to collect himself anew, taking his start from that incident on a plane of spiritual earnestness and love. Nevertheless, it remains true that the full harmony implied by the objective *logos* of the relationship is not reestablished before our friend has understood and admitted his wrong, until he has asked our pardon for it.

To insist on this condition is not to postpone but to uphold the value of peace. By so acting, we still keep aloof from strife. Our demand that our friend revise his conduct springs from our longing for an unsullied harmony and an enduring intimacy in our relationship with him; that is to say, for peace — perfect and undisturbed.

∾

We must deal prudently with violations of our rights

The safeguarding of peace presents an even more difficult problem when the offense in question is not merely one against charity — an act of unkindness or discourtesy, say — but an infringement of our rights, which we cannot refrain from defending. To take a few typical cases — somebody assumes a patronizing attitude toward us and would illegitimately restrain our freedom of decision, or is about to appropriate something that by rights belongs to us, or again, arrogates to himself certain claims on third parties who are really under our supervision: gives orders, for instance, which it is our exclusive right to issue, and the like. We cannot brook such things in all circumstances, let alone permanently; yet on the other hand, our insistence on our rights obviously entails the danger of dissension and conflict.

In such cases, we must begin by forming an unbiased view of the matter, so as to ascertain whether, objectively speaking, it is really we and not the supposed offender who is in the right, or whether the problem is not a complex one, with rights and wrongs in some way divided. On no account must we simply abandon ourselves to the natural automatism of our defensive reactions. Before deciding on our course, we must arrive at a detached judgment, which we should maintain as though it were not ourselves but a third party whose rights were encroached upon.

When, in our encounter with Christ, we have acquired an inward readiness to renounce the right thus challenged, should that be God's will, when we have performed the mental act of putting ourselves in our antagonist's place and envisaging the matter with roles reversed, as it were, and so gained the conviction that the right we attribute to ourselves is indubitably valid and not merely a putative one — then only have we created the necessary condition for taking action in defense of our claim, should further considerations lead us to do so.

Sometimes, the situation being unequivocal, it is very easy to arrive at such an impartial and sober judgment; in other cases it is apt to be more difficult. Having made sure, then, that our rights have in fact been interfered with, we must further examine before God whether the right in question is of such objective value as to justify us in risking peace in order to vindicate it. To a Christian, the mere fact that some right of his has actually been tampered with does not by itself constitute a ground for conjuring up the danger of strife. In many cases, it may be more pleasing to God that we renounce our legitimate claim; particularly, sometimes, in controversies concerning our material possessions.

On other occasions, however, it may be our duty to take up the challenge: thus, for instance, when somebody is bent on curtailing our legitimate freedom of decision.

In such cases we must oppose the encroachment, and therefore cannot shape our conduct with a view to avoiding a conflict at any cost. For our freedom is not ours to give away; it has been entrusted to us by God as an essential instrument for us to do His will.

∞

Even in conflict, we must desire peace

Still, whenever we have to defend our rights, we must do so in such a fashion that we avoid getting caught in the self-enclosed automatism of conflict. Steering clear of all irritation and malice, we must always preserve that inner freedom — that spirit of detachment — which looks upon everything in the perspective of God's will and of objective right, as though the rightful claims of an unidentified third party, and not one's own, were concerned.

As a first step, we should try amicably to persuade the offender to desist from his course; if this attempt fails, we should ask a third party to arbitrate the conflict. Again and again we should endeavor before God to evoke in ourselves that charitable attitude, free from all admixture of personal enmity, which makes us experience discord as a grievous thing.

Peace Begins Within Us

We ought never to think ourselves dispensed from the essential pursuit of peace — justified, that is to say, because of the unreasonableness of our adversary, in giving free rein to the autonomous dynamism of conflict and tolerating in ourselves an essentially inimical attitude toward him.

Every further step imposed on us by the aim of protecting our right should impress us with pain. We must never lose our awareness of a fundamental duty of charity in regard to the person in question.

Never, in particular, must the immanent evolution of the conflict (which, once set in motion, cannot be stifled so far as the objective order of events is concerned) come to determine our moral orientation. We must not be seduced into enjoying the wrangle or the blows we may manage to inflict on our antagonist. In other words, it is not enough that we ponder the matter before God at the beginning of the struggle, so as to decide whether we should embark upon it at all. During its entire course we must continue confronting ourselves with God again and again, lest its autonomous dialectic should become the law of our inward attitude.

Even though engaged in a conflict we could not possibly avoid, we must remain *lovers of peace*, who would at any time prefer a peaceful solution to a victory over the adversary obtained by means howsoever licit.

∞

We must avoid obsession with our rights

Notwithstanding the fact that in certain cases we are bound to defend our rights, we must never allow our mere displeasure at being threatened in some right of ours to become a motive of our conduct. There are people who feel upset by the fact alone that their sphere of rights is trespassed upon, although the offense referred to some good about which they care but little. Such a person will, for instance, if living in a tenement house, resent his neighbor's indulging in some noisy occupation (beating carpets, say) outside the hours legally reserved for such work, not because he is sensitive to noise, but in view of the disrespect for his rights involved in the thoughtless neighbor's behavior. Or again, it arouses his anger when a stranger takes his seat in a railway carriage, even though there be other empty seats nearby just as convenient.

Such people, then, jealously watch over the respect shown to their rights as such, independently of the interest they actually take in the good that their right happens to cover in the given case. The fact is that they attach an immense weight to the question of whether their person is treated with due esteem, which implies a scrupulous respect for their rights. Thus, if some property of theirs is stolen, they are much less grieved by the loss of that good than shocked by the sacrilegious interference with their range of rights. Hence, it does not lessen their fury if, owing to insurance, they suffer no material damage through the theft.

Something of this abstract sensitiveness about one's rights is present in practically all of us. The saints alone are entirely free of it. However, it is inconsistent with the *ethos* of the true Christian and should be diligently repressed. For, apart from its constituting a specific source of discord, it obviously harbors a residuum of proud self-assertion and of petty self-importance.

This attitude, again, must be precluded from contributing to the motivation of our conduct and tingeing our state of mind in cases when we are compelled to resist an aggression. Even should we deem it necessary to uphold some right of ours merely in order to curb the insolence of a reckless aggressor and prevent the establishment of a precedent that would place us in a false situation relative to him, we must remain inwardly free of that sensitiveness concerning our rights, and make our claim valid in a manner as though it were somebody else's.

∞

Cowardly acquiescence is not the love of peace

Of course, as has been pointed out above, a spineless disposition to abandon one's rights is no more in keeping with the true love of peace than is the obsession with one's rights as warned against here. Not to defend one's rights, out of sheer cowardice or love of comfort, has nothing to do with the true spirit of peace. For these chicken-hearted characters who would swallow any insult do not derive the principle of their conduct from a response to value; it is not the true value of peace that attracts them. They automatically obey the inclination of their nature, to which it comes easier to yield a right or to lose a possession than to sustain any conflict.

Not unlike a suggestible person who without critical reflection adopts alien opinions and outlooks just because he is exposed to their contact, these weaklings surrender anything for the asking, not on the ground of any conscious deliberation or of any reasoned conviction that would make them prefer surrender to strife as the lesser evil, but because they succumb to the dynamic superiority of others before they could even make an express decision. Such are the helpless "softies," pushed aside or exploited by anybody coming their way, incapable of opposing any resistance (independent of any question of value, nay, even of the question as to pleasantness and unpleasantness), a defenseless prey to any attack.

The kind of peaceable souls we have just been describing lack that basic response to value which is a prime condition for all true love of peace. They are unable, therefore, to ponder the essential problem as to whether their yielding does moral damage to the aggressor or not. For this, too, we must examine before God — in addition to the question as to the value of the threatened good — before we decide between offering resistance or abstaining from it for the sake of peace. Our renunciation may encourage the offender in his unrighteous course, and habituate him to disregard the rights of others to the detriment of many, and above all, of his own soul.

It is clear, then, that true love of peace cannot dispense us from fighting for our own rights. There is no commandment enjoining man to behave peacefully in all circumstances and to abstain invariably from struggle and strife. It can be our duty to defend some right of ours.

∞

Even in conflict, we must maintain inward peace

Yet, "blessed are the peacemakers"[7] implies two demands upon us: first, that we shall not decide to engage in a struggle unless, having examined the case in the light of God and in a state of full inward peace, we are convinced that it is our duty to uphold our right.

Secondly, it implies that even in the course of a conflict which we had to take upon ourselves, we shall abide in a state of inward peace; that our attitude shall always remain a detached one, undefiled by bitterness and rancor, connoting no enmity, but, on the contrary, charitable kindness toward our adversary; that we shall experience the conflict as a great evil, as a heavy cross we have to bear in pain.

In other words, so far as our state of mind is concerned, we must wage the conflict as though we waged it not. During all its phases, without ever allowing ourselves to be submerged by the blind automatism of strife, we must keep

[7] Matt. 5:9.

alive in us the longing for peace and, as far as our duty to fight permits it, the immediate readiness for peace.

∞

Peace may call for a struggle against evil

So much for the case where we must protect our rights against an aggressor. Let us turn now to the other type of situation: when we have to take our stand in defense of an objective value as such — in the supreme case, the kingdom of God itself. Here, evidently, to evade the struggle is much more difficult. For, mindful of the words of our Lord, "I came not to bring peace, but the sword,"[8] we should be soldiers of Christ. The holy Church on earth is called *ecclesia militaris* ("the Church militant"). We cannot at the same time hunger and thirst for justice — an inherent basic attitude of the true Christian — and be at universal peace with the doers of evil and the unjust. The meek St. John the Evangelist goes so far as to advise the faithful against greeting heretics.[9]

How are we to reconcile our character as a "soldier of Christ," who in St. Paul's words shall proclaim the divine

[8] Matt. 10:34.
[9] 2 John 1:10-11.

truth "in season, out of season," and intrepidly oppose or even combat evil, with our love for peace and our eagerness to avoid all strife?[10]

In order to solve this difficulty, we must first of all understand that an outward truce with evil — that is to say, a passive toleration of all objective wrongs, an attitude of silence and of letting things pass, which in some circumstances has the appearance of consent and sometimes actually results in consent — can never derive from a love for true peace. For the real value of peace resides in its being an outgrowth of love and an expression of genuine harmony.

The unison we pretend to establish with evil — the attitude of coolly allowing a power of wrong to unfold — neither rests on actual love nor reflects true harmony. Rather it is a product of weakness and involves a defilement with evil, a participation in the wrongdoer's guilt. Through our feeble submission to evil, we merely increase the disharmony that lies in evil as such and aggravate the discord that is implied in all evil, in all wrong that offends God: a discord deeper than the one implied in the sheer fact of conflict, however fierce.

[10] 2 Tim. 4:2.

Peace Begins Within Us

It is, on the contrary, our struggle against evil that must be recognized as a necessary consequence of a true love of peace, inasmuch as it also means a struggle against discord and an endeavor to limit its empire.

It is not in our power to prevent evil from raising its head at this or that point, but we must strive to restrict its reign within the narrowest limits possible or else we connive in its expansion and thus actually contribute to the evil of discord. God alone, not a peaceable behavior as such, is the absolute good. Our fight for the cause of God is necessarily also a fight for true peace, seeing that the latter coincides with the victory of the kingdom of God. Therefore, the spirit of peace which must animate a true Christian will never restrain us from fighting for the kingdom of God. It will determine a basic difference in quality between that fight and any merely natural conflict.

∞

Our struggle for the kingdom of God
must not be mixed with self-interest

In this context, again, a true Christian should first examine whether his zeal for the kingdom of God is not alloyed with some sort of personal interests, for that might easily be the case. Only too often, the fact that something objectively valuable is at stake provides us with a pretext for ruthlessly safeguarding our own interests on the strength of their incidental nexus with that higher cause. That is why it is necessary, before taking action, to consider the elements of the situation carefully before God — mistrusting our nature and the possible subconscious currents in our mind — and to probe our motives until we have gained a full certitude with regard to their character.

Be it understood: the fact that, in a given case, our struggle for the kingdom of God happens to converge with the line of our personal interests need not — nay, in certain circumstances, must not — prevent us from conducting that struggle to the limit of our forces. But neither must that fact be allowed to tinge in any way, to modify the quality of our combative attitude. We must carefully keep one thing apart from the other, and never for a moment stick the pretentious label of a *fight for the kingdom of God* on what is really an action meant to subserve our own welfare. In no wise must our pure, selfless, serene zeal for the kingdom of God be contaminated with the base coin of self-assertion.

Nor is that all. Even though we are standing for the kingdom of God, with no trace of personal preoccupations tarnishing our zeal — even though we are acting perhaps, in effect, against our personal interests — the *ethos* of our struggle might still be overlain with aspects that render it closely akin to a conflict waged on behalf of one's own interests but under high-sounding watchwords.

Thus, this is the case if we wage the fight for the kingdom of God after the fashion of a fight on our own behalf, making it *our cause* in a qualitative sense, conducting it, as it were, with the massive reaction of our nature. Many men, even good men, pursue an aim conceived purely in terms of objective value, simply because they have set it up as an aim and devoted themselves to it exactly as though some private and passionately desired aim were at stake. Entirely subject to the sovereign automatism of their formal purpose, they conduct the struggle with all their natural register of moods; with all the harshness, bitterness, irritation, and petulance of one who is bent on asserting himself.

∞

Love of peace demands charity toward sinners

To fight in this way is incompatible with a true love of peace. Our fight for the kingdom of God must be not only motivated but informed by our response to value lifted to a supernatural plane. Its spirit must be derived not from our own nature but from God. This will find its main expression in our constant endeavor to fulfill St. Augustine's[11] demand: "Kill the error; love him who errs."

While passionately combating an injustice, attacking a false doctrine, struggling to save a fellow soul, or pitting our forces against an expanding evil, we must never lose our living charity for the sinners and the misguided, but always remain solicitous about *their* good, too. Our very indignation, our tireless resistance, our stubborn advocacy of the good, our inexorable opposition to evil — these must, in all their phases, be permeated by the light of love and thus cleansed from all acrimony and fanaticism.

∞

*We must remain aware of the
dangers inherent in struggle*

The danger to be feared is that we might possibly assume such a truly Christian attitude when engaging in the struggle but desert it later, succumbing to the autonomous dynamism of hostility. That is why it is so important for

[11] St. Augustine (354-430), Bishop of Hippo.

the *soldier of Christ* again and again to actualize before God the meaning of his fight and to soften his heart in a supreme love for God, beholding his antagonists as brethren gone astray. He must always remain aware of the danger inherent in all fighting and never regard combative action as a neutral instrument which one may use freely if only it is ordained to an aim pleasing to God.

On the contrary, our activity with all its details must be altogether directed and colored by an ethical conception informed, in its turn, by our aim: the glory of God and the eternal welfare of our fellow men. This kind of fight must be widely different, not merely as regards its object but also as regards its formal character, from a fight waged in a natural spirit and destined to protect our interests.

In particular, we must guard against placing ourselves on a level with the adversary and from being infected with his spirit and morality. It must be an unequal fight — with a sharp contrast between his and our motives, principles, and methods. For our *fight for the kingdom of God* is by the same token a fight for true peace, whereas the fight of the children of the world is a fight for something that essentially implies strife and disharmony.

Making Christ's Peace a Part of Your Life

∞

The peace of Christ is inner peace

Two further supports must be mentioned on which to found the right attitude of a lover of peace engaged in fighting. One is patience;[12] the other is inward peace. The lover of peace preserves his patience while waging a struggle. He *lets God decide* whether he shall himself live to see that struggle crowned by victory; he conducts it without that violence which is the infallible mark of impatience. For he only fights in order to serve God and therefore with a complete detachment from self.

In accordance therewith, inward peace is the central condition for abiding by the spirit of peace in the midst of an indispensable struggle for the kingdom of God. Of this second dimension of peace we shall have to speak now: the peace whose possession is most necessary for the true Christian and to which Christ was eminently referring when He said: "Peace I leave with you; my peace I give unto you; not as the world giveth do I give unto you."[13]

[12] See Dietrich von Hildebrand, *Transformation in Christ* (Manchester, New Hampshire: Sophia Institute Press, 1990), ch. 12.
[13] John 14:27.

∞

True Peace Is Rooted in God

⚮

We shall only do justice to the full importance and value of peace if we realize that the peace Christ came to bring was, above all, inward peace. Let us state at once that here, too, apply both antitheses: that antithesis between peace and discord, and between true peace and false peace. The absence of all inward unrest is by no means invariably a good. It is a good on the condition only that it comes from a harmony with objective good and expresses a response to Truth. Sated contentment or a peace of mind due to thoughtlessness or illusion, is not a good but an evil — no matter how pleasant it may subjectively feel.

But it must be emphasized that this false peace differs radically from true inward peace objectively grounded, not only in view of its ultimate worthlessness but also as regards its experienced quality. The relevant question, then, is not: "How can we avoid all inward unrest?"; it is: "How can we find true inward peace?"

What we have said in reference to outward peace also holds true in the present context: not peace as such, but

God, is the absolute good. The only decisive question always remains this: "When are we united to God; when do we behave in a fashion pleasing to God?" And the distinctive high value of true peace lies primarily in the fact of its being the fruit of a true union with God and an expression of the right response to God.

∞

The value of an attitude depends on
its adequacy as a response to a good

The value of an attitude depends on whether it embodies an adequate response to a genuine objective good; to what is truly valuable in itself. Hence, it has to be judged by the two following criteria.

The important thing is, first, whether in a given case our will, our joy, our enthusiasm, our longing, and our love (or our sorrow, our indignation, our fear, and our repulsion) are each directed to an object to which such a response is proper and due. Malicious joy, delight taken in another's misfortune is bad; delight experienced at the moral progress of a fellow being is good. Enthusiasm evoked by an idol constitutes a negative value; as a response to a true good, it itself is a valuable thing. Moreover, it is from the object that the attitude derives not only its moral *sign*, but its distinctive note and quality. We know nothing definite about the specific quality of an act of love or of fear, of a mood of joy or enthusiasm, until we know the object to which it is directed.

∽

An attitude's value lies secondly in its consonancy with the hierarchy of values

The value-test of an attitude lies, secondly, in whether the intensity of our response, the role which an object plays in our soul's life, is consonant with the objective order of values. Thus, our joy about someone's conversion should be greater than our delight in a brilliant intellectual achievement.

Above all, what is intrinsically important or noble should delight us more than what is merely agreeable to us: for example, we should rejoice at having found God more than at having gained some earthly treasure.

Hence, it follows that so long as we have not found God, it is good for our spirit to be restless. Suppose the mere possession of earthly goods could satisfy us to the point of undisturbed happiness: this would mean a counterfeit happiness, a false harmony, and therefore a negative value. To be sure, earthly goods never can really gratify our longing;[14] but the illusion that they can do so is obviously worse than valueless.

∞

Inner peace is possible only in God

So long, then, as we are separated from God, as we have not found Him and are not reconciled with Him, we *should* have no peace. Blessed are the Advent souls, unsatisfied in the world, awakened to the truth that God alone can give us true peace, witnesses to St. Augustine's, "Restless is our heart until it reposes in Thee."[15] Unhappy, however, are the restless who find not God, although He has spoken to us; who flee communion with God; who refuse due response to the fact of our redemption by Christ.

∞

Those who are content in this world are farthest from God

We must not seek peace for its own sake, and on no account must we seek any and every kind of peace, but

---

[14] See von Hildebrand, *Transformation in Christ,* ch. 11.
[15] St. Augustine, *Confessions,* Bk. 1, ch. 1.

seek God and content ourselves with that peace which He alone can give our soul. Those restless in the world are nearer to God than those satisfied in the world. For the former at least take account of Truth insofar as they (in this fundamental sense) give the world the response due to it, and experience the objective evil of separation from God subjectively, too, as the evil it is. But they are unblessed insofar as they do not recognize the *whole* Truth, but pass by the true metaphysical situation of man — and, in particular, the radical change it has undergone owing to the Redemption — without yielding to it the right response.

Our transformation in Christ necessarily implies true inward peace. Yet, those are most remote from God who possess a false peace; those who, absorbed by purely terrestrial goods, are sated and content without God; those who smugly reject the knowledge that no creaturely thing can ultimately quench our thirst; those who escape being disquieted by the incertitude of the future and the impermanency of all earthly things, because they are too busy with the concerns of the moment ever to collect themselves at all. They live thoughtlessly as though this life were never to end; as though the warning which the holy Church addresses to us on Ash Wednesday,

"Remember, man, that thou art dust and unto dust thou shalt return," had no validity for them.

Some of them squander away their lives in shallow pleasures; others, again, are so engrossed in their daily concerns that, although not leading an agreeable life at all, they simply find no time to stop and think. The complete enslavement of their attention to the practical task immediately ahead deprives them of any leisure for feeling their want of peace. Like beasts of burden, they tread along their path in dull monotony, without ever becoming sufficiently awake to feel distressed by the meaninglessness of their lives.

∞

Those who sense the disharmony
of the world are closer to God

By comparison with them, who have peace in this sense, those who sense — and suffer from — the disharmony inherent in a world severed from God are by one degree nearer to the truth and thus to God Himself. Those who are searching restlessly and ceaselessly for true happiness; who are disappointed by every earthly pleasure or possession which would masquerade as an absolute; who are disturbed by the idea of death; who feel secure neither in themselves nor in the world; who face the future with anxiety, and are deprived of peace by their worry about whatever they love — they at least experience the insufficiency of a world grounded upon itself alone.

Just because they vaguely feel, without correctly interpreting it, the disharmony implied in their separation from God, they are no longer so widely separated from God as are those entrenched in a false peace.

∞

*Those who consciously suffer from
disunity with God are closer yet to Him*

Even closer to Truth are such as, while equally lacking peace, consciously and explicitly *trace* their want of peace to their disunity with God. Such are those who are not without belief in God, yet keep on doubting; who hear the call of God, but are reluctant to part with illicit joys; who are dragged to and fro between God and the world; who, held by the spells of sin, would yet wriggle themselves free; who, were it but possible, would fain serve two masters. These are the souls that most deeply *experience* disharmony, are most restless, and are most tormented by their knowing no inward peace.

Making Christ's Peace a Part of Your Life

The objective fact of their disunity with God is unquestionably a terrible evil, but the fact that it impinges upon their minds in the form of distress and anguish — robbing them of peace — is highly valuable, for it forces them into an awareness of Truth by one degree less indirect than is present in those who merely suffer from the immanent disharmony of the world without viewing it explicitly in terms of a disjunction from God.

They at any rate surmise the bliss that lies in a union with God; they recognize the seat of true peace and the central cause of their want of peace. They have taken profit from their trouble to the point of laying bare its real root. They have advanced as far as to evince an express yearning for God, although they still feebly evade a clear and unequivocal decision for God. Of such a kind was the tribulation St. Augustine suffered before his conversion, the unrest he described so movingly in his *Confessions*.

∞

*Inner peace comes only to him who
attains full reconciliation with God*

Inward discord, as we now see, is not an absolute evil, but an adequate response to the world taken in separation from God; it cannot and must not be overcome except by man's awakening to the Truth and his adequate response to the fact that beyond and above all the disharmony of the world, God the infinitely Glorious and Blissful One, who is Love, is enthroned. It will disappear when man becomes aware of his metaphysical situation, particularly as modified by Christ's Redemption of the world.

The nagging unrest of him who doubts and of him who writhes in the fetters of sin, the most deeply painful experience of unrest will dissolve as soon as he achieves an unequivocal surrender to God: peace will come to man when he lets himself fall into the arms of God and — submitting to the grace that makes him into a member of the Mystical Body of Christ, whose sins are washed away by the Blood of the Lamb — attains to a reconciliation with God.

Every one of us feels something of this same unrest, whenever he is aware of deviating from the paths which God has proposed to us; whenever his conscience warns him of a separation from God. No sooner do we turn back and renounce what has been separating us from God than our unrest commences to dissolve.

But until we have repented of our wrong and have been forgiven by God, our peace will not be completely restored.

Making Christ's Peace a Part of Your Life

∞

Inner peace requires a unified life ordered to goodness

The first and most obvious mark of inward peace, then, is a formal unity of our essential direction of life; an absence of different basic directions at loggerheads with one another; a liberation from unrest and incessant searching; the integral ordination of our interests and pursuits to an ultimate life-purpose.

But this formal unity — this inner coordination and convergency — is not all that inward peace implies. It also implies a unity with *the good;* a participation in the harmony implicit in the good as such. No matter how integrally (in a purely formal sense) we give our attention to what gratifies our pride and our concupiscence — without ever flinching from this our course; without being haunted by any pangs of conscience — we still live in a state of disharmony and can never taste true peace, which emanates from the intimate beauty of values.

All attitudes opposed to value carry in them a germ of discord, a principle destructive of community. In values alone dwells a unifying power. They alone, therefore, can fill us with true concord and harmony, which is a positive state of the soul, implying far more than a mere absence of instability or inward division.

True Peace Is Rooted in God

Clearly, nothing could be more unlike true peace in its quality than the state of mind characteristic of high pride. The proud man, self-contained and seemingly free from all inner contradiction as he may be, through his fierce contempt for objective values inevitably becomes tainted with the disharmony attached to all negation of the good.

∞

Inner peace also requires a personal relationship with God

Yet, even our participation in the good does not by itself give us what may *most properly* be called inward peace; for the latter requires our incorporation, not only in the realm of values and their harmony, but in *the living God*, in the holiness of the almighty Lord, who is the Good *per se* and who reveals Himself in Christ.

Inward peace, at its highest, means even more than our participation in the light of values, our reception of the tranquillity and simplicity conveyed by their power, our being integrally permeated with the tone of their accord and harmony. It means, beyond that, that clarity and limpidity of the soul which nothing except a real link, a personal communion, with the thrice Holy One can accomplish in the soul; that enlightening of which the prophet Isaiah says: "Arise, be enlightened, O Jerusalem: for thy light is come, and the glory of the Lord is risen upon thee."[16]

∞

True peace brings inner concord and unity

To sum up — true peace, the peace Christ means when He says, "My peace I give unto you," includes three main aspects.

First, a more formal one: a state of inner concord and unity takes the place of strife and division among conflicting orientations, of indecision concerning the ultimate directions of life. By contrast to an unappeasable disquietude — a fidgety groping for what might prove to be *the real thing* and the secret of true happiness — there is the valid recognition and enduring possession of the aim that makes life worth living; the state of resting in an ultimate which gives to everything else its meaning and renders all further search unnecessary. It is the attitude which fills the soul of Simeon when he exclaims: "Now Thou dost dismiss Thy servant, O Lord, according

[16] Isa. 60:1.

to Thy word in peace: because my eyes have seen Thy salvation."[17]

❧

True peace may only be founded on the highest good

The second main aspect of true peace refers to its *objective foundation*. The good in which we repose must be of a nature to justify this attitude of ours. It must in truth be the highest good: a good that, once found, really does render all further quest superfluous and inappropriate. This principle of objectivity — a general presupposition, strictly speaking, of all valuable attitudes in man — is what prints upon true peace the seal of validity and sets it apart from all kinds of illusory peace based on this or that deception. And the highest good, which alone can validate our peace, is also the only one that can *satisfy us completely*.

❧

Peace awakens us to values

Finally, true peace implies a *participation* in the immanent *harmony of values*. When truly at peace, we are

[17]Luke 2:29-30.

illuminated by the light irradiating from values; whereas our surrender to what panders to our pride and our concupiscence is bound to darken us inwardly. It is here that we touch the nerve of positive peace and gain sight of its proper quality.

By its incorporation and its habitation in the realm of values, the soul becomes, as it were, wide and luminous, soaring and lithe as these values. Its participation in the good opens it up to the unifying power of values, and thus infuses into it a new principle of unity and harmony.

The spiritually unprivileged — whether depraved or merely primitive or obtuse — and those entirely concentrated on what is gratifying to their desires, do not know this peace. They allow themselves to be filled by something that, notwithstanding the moments of pleasure it procures, is utterly devoid of this principle of intrinsic harmony, which liberates and at the same time collects the soul, takes all harshness and cloddishness from it, and adorns it with a luster of supple serenity. For what subserves the mere aim of gratification cannot give more than a dull pleasure, behind which lurks a sense of surfeit and inanity, and which renders us egocentric and heavy. The pursuit of mere subjective gratification condemns man to ever increasing emptiness and bluntness.

True Peace Is Rooted in God

∞

Wickedness is the antithesis of true peace

Even more glaring is the contrast between the last-described aspect of true peace and the inward complexion of the wicked who, in their spasm of pride, do not merely ignore the world of values in the sense of a blind indifference, but scorn objective value and defy God in an attitude of hatred and resentment. These unfortunates are ridden by what might be termed the counter-principle to peace; they carry in their souls a poison which represents a radical antithesis to the immanent harmony of values. They incarnate the spirit of discord and actually hate true peace: it might be said that they live *at war with true peace*.

Whereas the slaves to dull concupiscence may typify the state of a false peace, characterized by the absence of true *concordia* — of the luminous harmony inherent in true peace — the mental complexion of the proud haters of objective value (the state of mind epitomized, at its highest, by Satanism) embodies the qualitative opposite of true peace. Men of this kind absorb and assimilate as it were, the immanent disharmony of all typical negations of value, and appear incessantly to work at the decomposition of their own souls.

Making Christ's Peace a Part of Your Life

∞

True peace comes from communion with God

Yet, true peace, the peace of Christ, contains more than the harmony we owe to our participation in the realm of values: it connotes, as its consummation, that entirely distinct supernatural quality which arises from our *communion with God* alone, "through Him, with Him, and in Him."

Just as the world of the supernatural beauty of holiness towers high above all natural values — as a thing of unimagined novelty and greatness by contrast to even the highest natural beauty — so an unmeasurable gulf yawns between the immanent harmony of all values and the infinite harmony of Christ the God-Man.

Only think of the peace displayed by a lofty figure of antiquity like Socrates! Plato's[18] wonderful dialogue (the *Phædo*) portrays him, two hours before his death, peacefully meditating on the immortality of the soul, awaiting death in placid composure as the most important moment of life, serenely aware of the metaphysical situation of man (as far as it is knowable to our natural

[18] Socrates (469-399 B.C.), Plato (427-347 B.C.), Greek philosophers.

faculties), rejecting all suggestion of flight as injurious to the state. And compare with that noble sight the peace of the Christian saints! Francis of Assisi,[19] say, who, almost blind and his body on the verge of collapse, composed his jubilant *Canticle to the Sun;* or again, the behavior of the martyrs, facing a horrible death by torture, in holy peace and filled with celestial joy. Witness the epistles of Ignatius,[20] apostolic Father of the Church, or the record of St. Agnes's[21] words.

Different from all merely natural peace, however perfect, is the peace emanating from the saints: this blessed harmony entirely *sui generis,* this flowering of the supernatural life implanted in them by Baptism; this soaring peace resplendent with redemption and ringing with the note of victory over the world, which could never arise from their mere participation in the intrinsic harmony of values, but alone from their harmony with God the thrice blessed.

In close connection with the peace of such communion with God, we perceive one more mark of true peace,

---

[19] St. Francis of Assisi (c. 1182-1226), founder of the Franciscan Order.

[20] St. Ignatius (c. 35-107), Bishop of Antioch and martyr.

[21] St. Agnes, early Christian virgin and martyr.

which is a state of "being sheltered" proper to the soul that rests in the living God. In contradistinction to the metaphysical precariousness of the state of man left to himself, to the anxiety that must fill everyone who draws the full consequences from the concept of a world without God, to the fearful unrest oppressing one who has awakened to the metaphysical situation of man unreconciled with his Creator — and knows "how terrible it is to fall into the hands of the living God"[22] — he who is redeemed by Christ experiences that he is sheltered in God.

The world of values, the realm of impersonal ideas, cannot relieve us of the unrest that arises from our anxiety in facing the dark gate of death, from our concern about everything we love, from the irremediable insecurity of our fate. But he who takes shelter in the infinite love of a personal and almighty God may say with the psalmist: "But I have put my trust in Thee, O Lord. I said: Thou art my God; my days are in Thy hands."[23] He knows that God loves all those who are particularly dear to him infinitely more than he could love them himself;

[22] Heb. 10:31.
[23] Ps. 30:15-16 (RSV = Ps. 31:14-15).

that "the very hairs of their heads are all numbered."[24] He has received from our Lord's mouth the words: "Fear not, little flock, for it hath pleased your Father to give you a kingdom."[25]

Indeed, let us imagine even a condition in which no evil would threaten us any longer and in which we might eternally contemplate impersonal value; a condition like in the *Heaven of Ideas* which Plato puts before our eyes. Such a mode of being would still carry with it an ultimate note of forlornness and anxiety. In this apersonal world, we would still be abandoned to ourselves and closed up in our finiteness. We cannot be sheltered as finite persons, except in an infinite *Person*, who alone can fully comprehend us and lift us from the state of dereliction that is inherent in our finiteness. Only a personal face-to-face relationship with the infinite person of God can make us participate in infinite being. The almighty God alone can thus hold and sustain us so that we may say to Him: "Into Thy hands, O Lord, I commend my spirit."[26]

[24] Cf. Luke 12:7.
[25] Luke 12:32.
[26] Ps. 30:15 (RSV = Ps. 31:15).

∞

We Must Guard Our Inner Peace

∞

So much, then, for the essence and the aspects of true inward peace. Every living member of the Mystical Body of Christ, aware of Redemption and in the state of grace, possesses this true peace. Yet, although the redeemed are given peace in the basic metaphysical sense, on the plane of their human existence, they still may be inwardly torn and experience disharmonies.

∞

Deep peace may be disturbed by lesser disharmonies

Only a false response to our metaphysical situation can deprive us of peace essentially; but various false attitudes to purely creaturely things may still disturb the harmony and damage the peace of our souls. Even though the adequate basic response is firmly established in the concept and the conduct of our life, its victorious extension to all single departments thereof and the concrete realization of everything it implies will still mean a further ascent to higher religious levels. This is precisely the course we must follow in the process of our transformation in Christ; a course which also implies a strengthening and a qualitative enhancement of the basic response itself.

So long as we do not live integrally by Christ and in Christ, we may possess metaphysical peace to a certain degree and yet, on the plane of human relationships, suffer many disturbances of our concrete psychic peace, which may even adversely react upon the permanent state of our soul and diminish its harmony and integrity. Thus, it may happen to us to be torn between two great affections which, although neither of them is bad in itself, are yet incompatible with each other. Many a one, again, falls a prey to disharmony because he has chosen a career which is either altogether unsuitable for him or in which he does not feel in his right place.

There are, further, those who lapse into a state of inner discord as a consequence of having repressed a number of deeply stirring experiences instead of dealing with them in the clear light of consciousness and thus disposing of them as a source of trouble. Such persons often suffer from inferiority complexes or psychic spasms of various kinds. Their souls are caught in a state of disorder; they are full of inner contradictions. Their interior is darkened with unfreedom, lack of peace, and painful tensions. They torment themselves with unnecessary problems or fears. They feel, as it were, ill at ease with themselves; they are at odds with themselves.

As a specific factor of disharmony we may recall here that excessive self-observation — a reflective overconcentration on one's self, which prevents all true contact with the object and destroys the power of experience.[27] Persons of this type can never stop looking at themselves; they always contemplate themselves from the outside, as the central object in their field of vision, which they restlessly scrutinize now from one angle, now from another. Sufferers from hysteria furnish the most characteristic cases of this kind of disorder.

∞

Only surrender to God can heal lesser discords

This psychic lack of peace, too, can only be healed by forces derived from our surrender to God. To be sure, one can be originally free from the illness described above without being religious. There exists an unreflective, uncomplicated, "natural" kind of man, who, blessed

[27] See von Hildebrand, *Transformation in Christ*, ch. 4.

with a happy disposition and fortunate conditions of life, goes his way unhesitatingly without ever becoming a prey to that habitual psychic disintegration — although, adhering to a purely human plane he cannot (as we have seen) possess metaphysical peace.

But his is a harmony of a merely accidental kind, apt to collapse in the face of any serious test; nor can it, in a qualitative sense, be called true harmony at all, for the latter implies more than a mere absence of psychic disorder. This relaxed, healthy flux of life reveals at best the breadth, not the depth, of true harmony. Such persons are mostly childlike, deficient in consciousness; they are far from knowing the positive peace of an inward order and true simplicity.

Above all, there is no possibility for them to overcome inner discord, once it has arisen on a merely natural plane. There is no way back to a lost ingenuousness, childlikeness, or naturalness.

The disturbance evoked by conflicting experiences cannot be overcome except by confronting them with God (from which, as we know, results their effective confrontation with one another, too); by an attainment of full consciousness before the face of God, which renders even the most hidden chambers of our heart penetrable to the light of Christ — the serene light that clarifies and brightens up all things.

Whatever is cramped, repressed, entangled, or unsettled in us must be spread out before Christ and put up to His judgment, and hence receive its valid solution from *His* spirit. Our failure to examine and set right these things must be made good; whatever works mischief in the obscure corners of our soul must be brought to light and, as it were, be "shattered against Christ."

In the humble attitude of a surrender to God animated by supernatural love, all inner discord finds its solution. Then not only will all disharmony vanish, but true positive peace will become free to take up its home in the soul. It is the supernatural peace which flows from our "sharing in Christ," and which the Church in the Litany of the Sacred Heart calls "our peace and reconciliation"; the indestructible harmony derived from our resting in the victorious power and the all-pervasive light of Him by whose grace "night shall be light as the day."[28] Peace will then fill our soul without barrier or obstacle, lending it that serenity which is an unmistakable mark of the saints.

[28] Ps. 138:12 (RSV = Ps. 139:12).

Making Christ's Peace a Part of Your Life

In addition to the above-discussed *habitual* forms of our lack of peace, we must note certain more *transitory* forms. In these derangements we have to distinguish different elements.

∞

All heinous attitudes destroy peace of soul

We begin with the gravest one — that which constitutes a material, intrinsic antithesis to peace as actually experienced. What is meant here is a specific type of disharmony, distinct from the general aspect of disharmony which is inherent in all sorrow, pain, and displeasure, and which may engender lack of peace, but does not involve it of intrinsic necessity. (For one may feel a deep sorrow while being entirely at peace.) The disharmony we have in mind here bears a characteristically unhealthy note suggestive of inner strife and decomposition.

On the one hand, this note of decomposition may reveal a specifically *poisonous* tinge. This tinge belongs to morally reprehensible attitudes only, but not to all of them. It should not be confused, again, with the general aspect of disharmony attendant on all sin as such, which is a consequence of our separation from God and finds its expression in our guilty conscience.

We Must Guard Our Inner Peace

The specifically poisonous experience of disharmony which concerns us here is always present in a certain class of attitude, even though the subject may not evince a guilty conscience at all. It is a never-absent concomitant of hatred proper. All heinous attitudes exude, as it were, a venom which is responsible for this corrosive experience of disharmony. To be sure, the hater would apply that venom not to himself, but to the thing he hates; yet, whatever satisfaction he may derive from thus mentally injuring and corroding the object of his hatred, that venom inevitably affects — eats, as it were — his own soul. The state of mind into which we are driven by hatred, vindictiveness, envy, jealousy, or malicious pleasure necessarily embodies a radical antithesis to true peace — and that in a sense more specific than the one implied by sin and our separation from God as such. So long as we harbor this venom in us, we can certainly never attain true peace.

∞

Depression engenders disharmony in our soul
On the other hand, this note of decomposition may reveal a specifically *oppressive* tinge which accompanies all forms of the *depressive* states of mind. It need not

originate in any morally reprehensible behavior or intention. With its leaden atmosphere of gloom, it exercises a suffocating rather than a corrosive effect on our soul and our interior life. It might be compared to a kind of mildew blighting our entire mode of experience. Its action is, if not a poisoning, a palsying one — with the subject playing a much more passive part than in the case of disharmony issuing from hatred.

Whereas, in our heinous attitudes, we in a sense produce ourselves the venom whose toxic effects we cannot escape, the darkness of such depressive states of mind we suffer as an affliction imposed on us entirely from without.

Excitement and agitation disrupt our peace of soul

The second, more superficial, antithesis to inward peace consists in a formal — rather than intrinsic — derangement of our psychic order. It attaches to the various types of excitement or agitation.

By this we do not mean, of course, that inward tension which is inherent in every ordination to a future aim: that is, in every volition, in every anticipation of a joyous event, in all expectation and hope, in all longing

We Must Guard Our Inner Peace

and desiring. Tension in this sense, although it undoubtedly contains in contradistinction to the purely contemplative states of mind (such as the meditation of a truth, the delight taken in present beauty, or the experience of loving attention to a person) an element of unfulfillment, is not necessarily opposed to inward peace.

Even less do we mean by *agitation* that inward tension and intensity which goes with every keen, alert, or important experience, whether contemplative or active — as distinguished from relaxed states of mind, devoid of all stress of activity, whether purely immanent or transient, and best typified by recreation. The spiritual tension involved by all experiences in which high values move us or in which we respond to them — a tension that, far from disappearing, shall reach its apex in eternal beatitude — obviously implies no opposition whatsoever to inward peace. Rather, it belongs to the very consummation of that peace.

What we are speaking of, then, is agitation in the narrower and more trivial sense of the word, indicating a derangement of the psychic equilibrium and an interruption of the normal course of psychic life.

Insofar as agitation, in this sense, prevents us from a downward concentration, diverts us from contemplative attention, and hampers our pursuit of definite and permanent aims, it evidently interferes with our inward peace. It constitutes, not a material, qualitative, or intrinsic antithesis to peace as does disharmony proper, but at any rate a formal or structural one.

There are manifold varieties of agitation, too. It interferes with peace most manifestly when it takes the form of what we sometimes call *psychic agitation*: the specifically upset state of mind.

The quality of psychic agitation is an ultimate datum which we cannot reduce to anything else. It can only be grasped in an immediate experience. Its presence taints our whole vital rhythm with disorder. It is characterized by a thoroughgoing confusion, a sort of topsy-turvydom in the succession of our affective states. In the place of their normal nexus and progress, there prevails a tendency in the mind to swing to and fro without an aim: to flit impotently around one point, without arriving at a conclusion or achieving any result; to stick endlessly to one topic, or again, to buzz forth to a new one every moment.

We try spasmodically to flee from what is the cause of our agitation, only to return to it again and again from the most varying directions. Without mustering up

sufficient strength or courage to deal with it thoroughly
and sensibly, we yet constantly remain under its spell.

Moreover, the sufferer from this condition loses touch
with the outside world, with the objects and persons
that surround him. Not being able to shake off the spell
of the thing that excites him, he becomes incapable of
responding to the *logos* of a new task or situation. He
grows egocentric and apathetic. Imprisoned in a straitjacket, as it were, he can neither relinquish nor really
find his own self. In a word, he loses the capacity for
composure or recollectedness; and in such a disheveled
state of mind, when he has lost his head, he is liable to
display unpredictable, irrational reactions.

Sometimes we say of such a person that he is "beside
himself"; yet, we might not unreasonably call him locked
up within himself, for he certainly is the slave of a subjective concern. Anyhow, he is devoid of any adequate
perspective for the world of objects. In this state of alteration, we are faced with a specific form of depersonaliz-
ing obsession and inner enchainment.

In addition to it, there are other, more superficial,
forms of agitation, which are also opposed to inward
peace, but whose upsetting action is a more limited one.
For example, the agitation that grips one who is subject

to what is called a *paralyzing fear* — hypnotized, as it were, by the approach of the dreaded evil — or again, the kind of excitement, much more peripheral for all its explosiveness, which accompanies anger and impatience.

∞

Depression can paralyze the soul

Depression, further, which we have treated above as a source of intrinsic disharmony, also reveals an aspect of formal opposition to peace. Whether evoked by care and anxiety, by a humiliation, or by any situation apt to elicit a feeling of inferiority, depression not only impedes the qualitative experience of peace as such, but also entails a formal disorder in psychic life, not identical with, but in some ways similar to the one due to agitation.

He who labors under a severe depression will exhibit, not the specific fitfulness and unrest of agitation, but a similar tendency to evade dealing with the cause of his trouble in conscious clarity, and to let himself be possessed by it in an illegitimate fashion.

He, too, is stuck to something — not in the sense of circling around it restlessly, but in the mode of torpor and stagnation. He, no less than the excited type, loses touch with things and persons, and becomes egocentric, without, again, finding himself or preserving an adequate view of his experiences and aims. To him, too, we might apply the simile of the straitjacket. Or, since in him the place of a senseless and spasmodic activity is taken by a morbid passiveness, we might vary the metaphor and describe him as a person living under a glass cover. An experience — a blow, an impression, a situation — which he has not been able to digest sticks, as it were, in his throat. In his paralyzed state, he cannot get over it, nor advance further. Resilience, hope, and confidence are stifled in him.

∞

Material and formal elements of
disharmony sometimes combine in us

Both types of *actual* or *psychic* lack of peace — the intrinsic and the merely *formal* one — imply that some aspect of an experience or an event acquires a subjective emphasis out of proportion with its true significance. The subject accords to it a place in his life which is in no way justified by its objective content.

As we have noted in the context of depression, the derangement of our inward peace may combine, in the concrete case, the material aspect of qualitative disharmony with the formal one of an immanent disorder among the subject's mental concerns. In fact, this is what happens most frequently. But that is no reason for abandoning the clear distinction between the two types of psychic factors militating against inward peace.

With regard to this double aspect, *psychic* or *actual* peace presents a clear analogy with the *habitual* or *super-actual* one. Just as habitual peace is characterized by a formal and a material element — simplicity and unity on the one hand, the soul's participation in the qualitative harmony of the Good on the other — actual peace, in its turn, admits of a distinction between its formal and material sides: of an immanent psychic order, as opposed to the disorder of agitation; and again, the quality of intrinsic harmony as opposed to the note of disharmony, be it of a virulent and poisonous or of a leaden, dismal tinge.

∞

Outward factors may also disturb our inner peace

Now as to the various outward factors that may, even though we be habitually at peace, disturb our peace on the plane of *actual* psychic life, these are, generally speaking, evils which have befallen us or which threaten us:

more particularly, cares or preoccupations of all kinds. The proper root of the disturbance, however, always lies in a false mental attitude within ourselves which allows these outward factors to act upon us disproportionately or lures us into opposing them with exaggerated or irrational reactions.

A threefold division commends itself here. Our inward peace may be marred, first, by an attitude which in itself is morally reprehensible, such as envy, hatred, jealousy, or, at a different level of relationships, impatience.

It may be interfered with, secondly, by responses which are not in themselves condemnable, nay, which in the context of a purely natural outlook appear rational and justified; which, however, in view of an interpretation of the universe as derived from Revelation, and particularly of the consequences of the Redemption, imply, on man's part, an inadequate response to his essential situation. Especially, the manifold varieties of fear and dread fall into this class.

A disturbing effect may also issue, thirdly, from responses which in themselves are not only justifiable but even necessary, and also retain their legitimacy if confronted with Revelation and Redemption, but which need correction or modification, for they contain a kind

of sting and are, until that sting be removed, apt to upset our inward peace. Distrust, indignation, and sorrow,
as well as the consideration of fighting for a good cause,
enter into this category.

∞

Inner peace may be overthrown by
reprehensible attitudes such as jealousy

Let us take these three groups of peace-destroying
factors in turn.

First, those emotional reactions which are open to
moral criticism: the most important case, here, is that of
jealousy. We do not mean jealousy in that broader sense
of the term in which it is not deserving of reproach at
all — the pain one necessarily feels when a beloved person ceases to reciprocate one's love; a pain that is likely
to be increased by the fact of that person's transferring
his or her affection to another — but jealousy in the
stricter sense.

What we mean is a bitter, irritated, malignant attitude linked to the situation of personal rivalry. In all its
manifold forms — whether it refers to a rival's success
or fame, the preference accorded him by a third party, or
the fact that a person whose love we covet leans toward

him instead of responding to us — jealousy constitutes an egocentric attitude.

The jealous man measures himself with another, begrudging his rival — in rebellion against the dispensation of God — what he would fain have himself. Rivalry as such is what specifies jealousy — the fact that, apart from being displeased with our lack of a certain good, we feel irritated by another's possessing it.

Jealousy includes, then, both the simple distress over being deprived of the good one desires — or, more exactly, a peevish and sullen kind of reaction to this evil — and a specific interest in having no one else possess that good either: the aspect of competition and rivalry. Thus, in the case of infidelity on the part of a beloved person, our jealousy never fastens upon the unfaithful person alone; it also attacks the successful rival. We seek to humiliate, to depreciate, to confound our rival in some fashion. We view him with unfriendly eyes and delight in any self-exposure into which he may blunder.

Now jealousy, whether groundless or "justified," always connotes a specific unrest. Aimlessly and endlessly, the jealous one revolves around one theme. He keeps a constant watch over the behavior of the object of his jealousy, prying into his movements with insatiable curiosity; he is astir with irritation, and his life is poisoned by a distinct kind of unrest.

To sum up, jealousy is opposed to peace in a twofold sense. On the one hand, it reveals a poisonous tinge of disharmony, qualitatively inconsistent with peace. On the other, it reveals the typical alteration which we have called a *formal* opposition to peace: the state of swinging to and fro and of circling around one point, the loss of contact with the universe of objects, and so forth.

Envy differs from jealousy in that it is opposed to peace because of its aspect of poisonous disharmony only; it does not imply the specific marks of a structural disintegration of psychic life. It is the same with hatred, "malicious joy," and similar attitudes. Against this must be said, however, that hatred, envy, and malicious pleasure display the note of poisonous disharmony to a much higher degree than does jealousy, as they involve a greater moral fault than jealousy does, and separate us more sharply from God. Only from the specific point of view of actual or psychic derangement of peace does jealousy present a particularly typical case.

Now, jealousy is one of the things that cannot subsist before the face of Jesus. Whenever it raises its head within us, we must take care immediately to disavow and to uproot it. It must be "shattered against Christ," as it were, dissolved by the glance of His love. Thus will the peace, too, which it has driven away, return to our mind.

The case of jealousy presents some analogy with that of impatience, although the latter interferes with peace in a more purely formal and far more superficial way. Impatience as such entirely lacks the aspect of virulent disharmony. The unrest it evokes, although apt to be very drastic in a sense (no other emotion, except anger, makes one so quickly lose one's self-control), does not exhibit the specific marks of what we described above as psychic alteration. It has much less tendency to work a destructive effect in the depths. Its very explosiveness is linked to its transient character. Withal, impatience constitutes a typical and irksome danger to outward peace.[29]

∽

Inner peace may be upset by fear or anxiety
Among the second class of factors that may upset our peace of mind, fear — or, more precisely perhaps,

[29] See von Hildebrand, *Transformation in Christ*, ch. 12.

anxiety — ranks foremost. Anxiety is not, by itself, a false and immoral response. There are things we justifiably fear or dread; nor is there anything intrinsically evil about anxiety. It does not, therefore, carry within it what we have attempted to characterize as poisonous disharmony; yet it is associated with that leaden tinge of disharmony which, as we have seen, belongs to the graver states of depression.

Above all, anxiety impinges on our peace in the sense of its formal or structural derangement. There are kinds of anxiety which plunge us into a state of alteration: what may, in particular, exercise such an effect is the torturing vague fear of some uncertain or indeterminate but grave evil: take, for example, our concern about a beloved person of whom, without being able to account for the delay, we have had no news; or again, our fear lest we should lose the affection of a beloved friend.

Such anxieties may bring in their trail all the disturbances characteristic of psychical alteration. Furthermore, there is a specific variety of paralyzing fear. When seized by this, we stare at the approaching danger in a helpless state of numbness, like a bird hypnotized by the cat poised to jump.

We Must Guard Our Inner Peace

Now, as has been hinted before, anxiety, justified as it may be in the world, became a false response after the Redemption of the world by Christ. "In the world you are afraid: but be of good cheer, I have overcome the world."[30] A true Christian must no longer abandon himself to oppressive or benumbing anxiety. He must conquer it with the weapon of his confidence in God; his consciousness that nothing can separate him from the love of Christ — in the spirit of the psalmist, saying: "For in Thee, O Lord, have I hoped: Thou wilt hear me, O Lord my God."[31] He must endeavor to rise above his anxiety with the strength derived from his resignation to the will of God, from the virtue of hope, and from his awareness of being sheltered in the Divine Love. Thus will he regain the peace he has lost through anxiety.

∽

Inner peace may be disturbed by legitimate responses

In regard to the third type of peace-disturbing factors, the situation is vastly different. Mistrust; indignation; the struggles we inevitably have to face on earth;

[30]John 16:33.
[31]Ps. 37:16 (RSV = Ps. 38:15).

the manifold forms of sorrow and pain that beset us in this valley of tears — here are attitudes and states of mind which have not been rendered invalid even by the Redemption. And yet they, too, may — if we abandon ourselves to their autonomous strain — dislodge our inward peace.

∞

Necessary mistrust may threaten our peace

In particular does this apply to mistrust. Whenever we grow to mistrust a person and start to look behind all his actions and utterances for something different from what they pretend to mean, a specific form of peacelessness is likely to arise in us. We are searching restlessly for something hidden. We tentatively interpret that person's behavior along varying and contradictory lines. We fall a prey to constant doubt, which cannot but make us prejudiced and diminish our freedom. Our primary, basic contact with the person in question becomes envenomed and atrophied.

This may easily impair our attitude of openness to our fellow beings in general, and, as it were, throw us back on ourselves. We may thus become wrapped up in ourselves and develop traits of egocentrism. The habit of observing the person we mistrust from the outside, from a remote point of vantage, with the resulting compulsion to decipher his every gesture and expression, impregnates our mind with a sense of insecurity most adverse to peace, and interferes with the healthy rhythm of our psychic life.

Yet, in various situations we have to be mistrustful, lest we should be deceived and our confidence abused. Within the framework of terrestrial life, it is not permissible for us to indulge a debonair confidence in everybody and everything, glibly putting aside all mistrust, merely in order to avoid the oppressive experience of not being able to *expand* freely, unchecked and unreserved.

For man to insist upon this is definitely illegitimate; in fact, it amounts to a form of easy-going indolence and self-indulgence. The truth is that again and again, life places us in situations in which we can hardly afford not to mistrust people. However, we must learn how to do so in a fashion not impairing our inward peace.

∞

God helps us examine our mistrust

To begin with, we must in general train ourselves not to have our equilibrium upset by every outward disharmony. We should firmly avoid depending on a naturally harmonious situation and presupposing it as a matter to be taken for granted. God and His kingdom, the eternal happiness that is our goal — these are to constitute the pivot of our life and the indestructible source of our inner harmony.

As for this valley of tears, we must in our general outlook reckon with its inherent disharmoniousness. The basic answer thereto is contained in the psalmist's words: "My heart is ready, O God."[32] So long as our center of gravity lies in God, no outward disharmony — although we may not separate suffering from its effect — will be able to unsettle our balance.

If, whenever we perceive in us the germs of mistrust, we at once proceed to collect ourselves in God and to spread out the whole situation in His light; if we thus wake into awareness of reality in the proper and eminent sense (supernatural reality) and revive our affiliation to that reality — then the object that has aroused our mistrust will, on the one hand, lose its power to trouble our equilibrium, and on the other, reveal to our eyes its comparative insignificance in the scale of universal being.

[32]Ps. 107:2 (RSV = Ps. 108:1).

We Must Guard Our Inner Peace

We must then carefully examine in the sight of God whether our mistrust is in fact objectively grounded and not perhaps a mere outgrowth of a mistrustful disposition on our part. If, in the light of such an examination, it proves to be warranted, our task will next be to keep it within the limits of its objective justification. We must not start doubting everything, but on the contrary, must stand firm against the lure of glib generalization. In brief, we must resist being carried away by the automatism of mistrust. We must endure the suffering that results from our being thus disappointed in someone, rather than seek to ease it by simply withdrawing our love and separating ourselves from that person.

Our endeavor should be to rise above the situation, and, instead of having our attitude imposed by the behavior of our partner, consider him in a spirit of merciful love, observing at the same time the necessary caution. We must not allow ourselves to be thrown back upon ourselves, nor get immured in ourselves.

Most of all should we guard against the extension of such a state of mind to our general attitude, beyond the limits of our relations with the offender himself. In other words, what we ought to do is to confine our mistrust within the limits of its objective validity, thus subordinating it to the teleology of our life rather than permitting it to control the latter.

We should also strive to incorporate that objectively necessary mistrust in a comprehensive attitude of charity, and so have it shaped by the supremacy of love rather than have our mental complexion defiled with a heinous tinge.

If we have thus circumscribed and tamed our distrust — without, until the grounds for it disappear, suppressing it — the destruction of our inner peace will be prevented or repaired, even though we shall still be afflicted with the residuum of pure and venomless chagrin.

∞

Sorrow may darken our inner peace

However, a deep sorrow itself, while it never bears that specific note of peacelessness which marks the unchecked raving of mistrust, may darken our inner peace. Sometimes a person stricken with real grief will revolt against his misfortune. Unable to digest it and to pass on, he will cleave to his grief and, owing to his oppression by it, become paralyzed in all his vital functions. When the sorrow leads to despair or to expostulation with God, a climax of inner peacelessness is attained.

We Must Guard Our Inner Peace

It is utterly false to hold that we ought *not* to sorrow over a real misfortune.[33] Any attempt to evade the cross, be it by a mental technique of dulling ourselves to pain or by fostering in ourselves the illusion that we are, essentially, no longer in the valley of tears but in the realm of eternal happiness, is hopelessly mistaken. We should not try to overleap suffering.

True, Jesus by His Crucifixion has redeemed the world and cleansed all suffering from its poisonous sting. Yet, Jesus also spoke the words, "If any man will come after me, let him deny himself and take up his cross."[34] The cross awaits us inescapably on our life-path; and we have to accept it. We should, however, take it in imitation of Christ, and endure all suffering in the spirit of Christ, in Christ, and with Christ. If governed and shaped by those two eminently Christian attitudes of mind — resignation to God's will, and patience — all suffering will become transfigured and pleasing to God.

[33] See von Hildebrand, *Transformation in Christ*, ch. 16.
[34] Matt. 16:24.

∞

Peace Is Essential to Happiness

∞

Patience in general, is, of course, implied in the virtue of acquiescence to God's will. Full subordination and surrender to God's absolute kingship contains an inward assent to everything that faces us inevitably and is thus the result of a decree or at least a permission of God. "My Father, if it be possible, let this chalice pass from me. Nevertheless, not as I will, but as Thou wilt."[35]

In these words of Jesus, all aspects of our right attitude to pain are condensed: the subordination of all our desiring and longing to the will of God; our recognition of His absolute mastery, which bids us say at every joyful or sorrowful event, "Behold the handmaid of the Lord: be it done to me according to thy word";[36] our response to the infinite wisdom of God, who says to us, "My ways are not thy ways";[37] our awareness of the infinite glory of God and of the sublime fact that whatever has been

[35] Matt. 26:39.
[36] Luke 1:38.
[37] Isa. 55:8.

accomplished expresses a decree or at least a permission of the holy will of God; and finally, our knowledge that "all turns to bliss for those who love God."[38]

Here is, in a word, resignation to God's will — a thing impossible except as a response to the concept of the universe that is conveyed to us by Christian Revelation. It does not dissolve suffering, but it transfigures suffering and removes from it that sting which threatens to destroy our inward peace. It prevents us from remonstrating with Providence. Resignation to the will of God — our total surrender of self to God and His infinite love; our knowledge of being sheltered in Him, "through Him, with Him, and in Him" — this, above everything else, is what strips all worries and evils of their power to disturb our peace.

∞

Depression can be diminished by
patience and resignation to God's will

It also plays a decisive part in our mastering of depression and the specific lack of peace it entails. Whenever something that is not a true evil but merely appears as

---

[38] Cf. Rom. 8:28.

such to our pride or our inordinate covetousness preys on our mind, we must attempt before Christ to uproot from our soul this unfounded sensitivity. The depression and its peace-disturbing effect will disappear when we succeed in dissolving before the face of Christ this illegitimate field of susceptibility. No doubt, this may often prove a laborious task, and require a long ascetical training. Yet, it is the more necessary because in this case — just as with jealousy, and particularly with hatred — the attainment of inner peace is closely linked to the victory over an actual moral defect in us.

If, on the other hand, the cause of our depression *is* a true evil, what we should do is not to try to banish it from our consciousness, conceal it from ourselves, or explain it away — and so provide it with a harmful subconscious hold on our mental life — but to set it clearly and consciously, confronting it with Christ, in the place that is objectively due to it within the universal framework of reality. We must then try to accept it consciously and expressly in an act of resignation to the will of God.

If we thus receive that evil as a cross from the hands of Christ, submitting to it expressly — taking it upon us actively, as it were, rather than merely enduring it in passive helplessness — it may still hurt no less, but it will no longer weigh us down, no longer affect us as a paralyzing poison, no longer warp our peace of mind. Finally, as regards future evils whose incidence is still uncertain, we must lay them in the hands of God, and from Christian resignation and confidence in God, derive, in reference to those specified menaces, too, the attitude thus expressed in St. Paul's words: "Be not solicitous,"[39] or in the psalmist's: "Cast thy care upon the Lord."[40]

∞

We must bear the burden of care, but strive to retain our inward peace

This is not to say that we do not have to bear the burden of concerns about future evils. Some people are inclined to shut out and pass over such concerns in a false way. They ease their consciences with the happy formula of "confidence in God," whereas in fact they are just easy-going, and intent on avoiding unpleasant matters as long as they can possibly manage it.

---

[39] "Be not solicitous; but in everything, by prayer and supplication, with thanksgiving, let your petitions be made known to God" (Phil. 4:6).
[40] Ps. 54:23 (RSV = Ps. 55:22).

Peace Is Essential to Happiness

We should, in truth, accept all burdens that God imposes on us, including the burden of care. We should, accordingly, prepare for all trials we see coming, and, so far as it is within our power, try to avert an evil not yet accomplished. However, the acceptance of this burden must not take away our peace. If in a general sense we acquiesce in bearing our cross; if we succeed in getting rid of the tenacious, secret resistance of the *old man* in us against everything that hurts our nature; if we are ready to receive everything God has meted out to us as a gift of His love and a means of our sanctification; if we surrender all *self-evident* claims to happiness and shake off the illusion that even on earth a state of undisturbed bliss might, after all, be attained — then we shall be able to face the threat of approaching evils, too, without losing our inward peace.

No sane man will deny it to be implicit in our terrestrial situation that the threat of great evils which close in upon us — when we have reasons to apprehend, say, the loss of a beloved person — should afflict us with anguish and care; nor are these compatible with a state of unruffled calm and unimpaired peace. Yet, in the midst of all the inevitable alarm, in our deepmost soul, we can and must preserve that serene peace which flows from our surrender to God's will and our firm belief that "God is love."[41]

∞

We must remain recollected in the midst of cares

Another condition, too, has to be fulfilled so that amidst all the tribulations of life, we may safeguard our inward peace. We must maintain a *recollected* mode of life.[42] If, indeed, we conduct a bustling and fitful sort of life with one aim chasing the other, involving a breathless succession of disparate tensions — a sort of life which never gives us time to pause and to meditate, nor allows any possibility of a contemplative attention to God — we shall be exposed to incessant derangements of our peace.

How could we, amidst the turmoil of such a life, develop the habit of confronting everything with God and of thus subjecting all our single preoccupations to an intrinsic order? How could we dwell in the depths of reality and the realm of eternal values? How could we find ourselves?

[41] 1 John 4:8, 16.
[42] See von Hildebrand, *Transformation in Christ*, ch. 6.

Peace Is Essential to Happiness

On the contrary, pushed about and unduly possessed by our rapidly alternating tasks (all of which carry in them the impetus of urgency), we are at the mercy of the autonomous mechanism of each in turn. In our constant attention to present and fugitive actuality, even should the matter in hand be ever so profound and important in itself, we are hopelessly incapable of setting ourselves, in the light of God, at a distance from all things, including our own ego.

Yet, this distance, as has been shown, forms an indispensable prerequisite for the neutralization of any kind of depression and excitement.

Even aside from this, a hyperactive and one-sidedly pragmatic rhythm of life — in which contemplation is doomed to wither — involves as such, in a general sense, a certain formal lack of peace. The restlessness, the speed, the nervous fatigue inherent in such a mode of life, the feverish rhythm of work and the bondage to the imperative of doing that are inseparable from it, inevitably plunge man into a state of peacelessness.

This is not the peacelessness of disharmony or of a subverted equilibrium (which is the note, for instance, of jealousy), but at any rate the peacelessness of a peripheral, centrifugal mode of being, of an endless rushing and routing. It, too, forms an antithesis to positive peace. Such bundles of energy, bursting with dynamism and delivered up entirely to the concern of the moment, who can never allow themselves a spell of emerging from the immanent logic of their activities, essentially carry with them a suggestion of peacelessness. Not for them is the state of "recollectedness." True peace, then, is inseparable from recollection.

∞

Composure is not the same as recollection

Composure of mind, of course, seems to be possible without true peace. There are people who manage their affairs slowly and comfortably, without any hustle and bustle at all, and who nevertheless cannot be described as being truly and inwardly at peace. But such people, although the slow cadence of their vital manifestation creates an impression of calmness and composure, are too indifferent, empty, or irrelevant to be really recollected.

What matters in this regard is not the quick or slow cadence of one's reactions, nor the tense or relaxed quality of one's vital rhythm. It is, rather, the presence or absence of concentration and contemplation; one's tendency toward the *depths* or the *periphery*; whether one's attitude of mind tends to be reflective or dissipated; whether one lives in a mode of unity and continuity, or as a puppet actuated, from moment to moment, by the heterogeneous flux of events, impressions, and aims — a slave of imperious automatism. Such automatism may be seen, too, when we engage too readily in a great variety of work, even though all the activities we embark upon be in themselves legitimate.

∞

We must have our spiritual roots in God

The true *actual* peace of the soul depends, finally, on that *superactual*, habitual, constant attention to God, that sustained consciousness of having our roots in God, which allows our interior world to be penetrated by a ray of His infinite peace. This conveys to us a foretaste of ultimate harmony and protects us against inward disunity and unrest.

It is implied in this true peace that we shall never be wholly submerged by the vortex of successive tensions which we have to endure. We shall never so forget the true and perennial order of things as to overestimate the task of the moment merely because we are caught in the tension of our effort to realize it.

Making Christ's Peace a Part of Your Life

∞

Lack of inner peace renders happiness impossible

Lack of peace constitutes a threefold evil. First, if experienced as such, it is essentially inconsistent with true happiness — most of all, the lack of peace associated with alteration and with depression. It is not, of course, in our power to eschew all unhappiness. On earth, no human being can escape the cross. And particularly, no Christian: even should he be spared all trials in his personal life, he would still suffer from the multiform manifestations of that basic disharmony which is a consequence of Original Sin. But, provided that we give God the right answer, it is in our power to avoid peacelessness.

Moreover, man's longing for true happiness — nay, for a blissful life — is something that God has implanted in the heart of everyone, and so we are justified in looking upon any unhappiness which we have ourselves guiltily caused as a veritable evil, a thing that ought not to be.

Apart from other reasons, then, we should shun whatever is opposed to peace inasmuch, also, as it constitutes a poison for our happiness, a subjective evil of which we are legitimately anxious to rid ourselves.

Peace Is Essential to Happiness

∞

Lack of peace is at its root an insult to God

The second and more important reason why lack of peace means a real evil consists in the insult to God which lies at its root. This is most patently true in regard to the type of peacelessness that springs from attitudes immoral in themselves — such as hatred, envy, or jealousy — which fill us with the poisonous disharmony proper to them.

Here our lack of peace is plainly caused by an attitude that insults God and separates us from Him. Our peacelessness represents a symptom of the disease which has befallen our soul. It is a product of the sinful attitude which in objective reality separates us from God and which therefore cuts us off from the source of all peace.

In its other forms, too, our loss of inward peace always presupposes some devious attitude on our part. It always indicates a state of mind in which we fail to give the proper and adequate response to the situations and events we are faced with, and in particular, a failure to respond to everything according to what it is and means in the light of God. Such is, as has been shown, the central defect that underlies all disorders of our inward peace.

Making Christ's Peace a Part of Your Life

∞

Lack of inner peace separates us from God

And finally, not only does our lack of peace originate in some cause that isolates us from God; in its turn, it reaffirms and increases our separation from God. It constitutes a formal obstacle to our full awareness and loving contemplation of God, to our delight in His infinite beauty.

By contrast to the above-discussed second aspect of peacelessness, this third one is most clearly visible in cases where the root of our lack of peace is not an expressly evil attitude — not one that would by itself banish us far from the face of God. Whenever, for instance, we fall a prey to anxiety degenerating into a state of depression or alteration, this condition will in a purely formal sense prevent us from reposing in God, and make us incapable of mental prayer as well as of every genuine act of contemplation.

For one thing, we are too much possessed by what depresses or agitates us to be capable of an adequate attention to God. In general, as has been pointed out, we are then cut off from all contact with the universe of objects. Furthermore, the unhealthy condition of our vital rhythm prevents us from recollecting ourselves and from all concentration toward the depth of our being. Lack of peace, then, is a disease of the soul which shuts us off from what is outside the ego and thus in a purely formal sense separates us from God.

∞

Lack of inner peace separates us from other persons

Nor does it separate us from God only. It also makes us unable to attend to other persons according to the will of God. And so, inasmuch as it renders us egocentric, our lack of peace also causes us to offend against charity.

Under its action, we become indifferent and lose the capacity of adequately dealing with the multifarious tasks which life imposes on us. It saps our working-power and undermines our faculty of coordination. It makes us scatterbrained and is thus responsible not only for many omissions but for many mistakes on our part.

Lastly, it also diminishes our readiness to keep peace with others. Our inner state itself being peaceless, any attack or insult on the part of others — be it even a merely putative one — will easily provoke us to a heated reaction and thus lure us into discord and conflict.

Nor can we, in such a condition, conduct a struggle for the kingdom of God except in a mode of rancorous irritability unworthy of the cause. For this great task in particular, so difficult to pursue without increasing the amount of strife in the world, inward peace constitutes a strict formal condition.

Therewith we return to our starting point. In order to preserve the spirit of peace and our love for peace in the midst of that struggle for the kingdom of God which we have to wage as a soldier of Christ in this passing world, there is (apart from the virtue of patience) no precondition equal in importance to this one: that we ourselves possess true inward peace and keep it intact throughout the struggle.

∞

Inner peace is possible only for those who
give themselves unconditionally to Christ

To be sure, the significance of true inward peace is not limited to its being a condition for outward peace. It constitutes a high good in itself. Indeed, it is so intimately linked to our transformation in Christ that it cannot, in the midst of all the threats to it, fully and sustainedly unfold except in such as have given over their souls to Christ.

This can be affirmed in reference to each single aspect of inward peace as analyzed in the foregoing pages.

Peace Is Essential to Happiness

In him alone who really and truly prefers nothing to Christ; whose life is shaped and remodeled by a total surrender to Christ; who follows Christ "leaving everything behind"[43]; who is undivided and unhampered by any inward resistance in belonging with all his soul and will to God (whose property, to be sure, we all are in metaphysical fact) — in him alone who is thus turned toward God and incorporated in Christ may the inexpressible sweetness of the peace of Christ, which in St. Paul's words "surpasseth all understanding,"[44] spread out in all its wealth, undisturbed by any accidental agents of disorder.

He alone who has established in his heart the words of the Lord, "Seek first the kingdom of God,"[45] and who no longer hungers and thirsts for anything but justice (that is, ultimately, Christ), possesses that supreme freedom which permeates his soul with true inward peace.

True peace only blossoms out of a life entirely rooted in Christ and illumined by the light of Christ; of the experience of having tasted the untellable sweetness

[43] Cf. Luke 5:11.
[44] Phil. 4:7.
[45] Matt. 6:33.

of Him whom the holy Church thus glorifies in Her chant:

> Jesus, the very thought of Thee
> With sweetness fills the breast;
> But sweeter far Thy face to see,
> And in Thy presence rest.

Of that supernatural inward harmony, which nothing can destroy anymore, he alone partakes whose heart has been wounded by Jesus and molten in His love; who is drunk with the sweetness of His love, and able to sing with the Church:

> No voice can sing, no heart can frame,
> Nor can the memory find,
> A sweeter sound than Jesus' Name,
> The Savior of mankind.

It is the Holy Spirit — "rest for the weary, refreshment for the pining, solace in the midst of woe"[46] — who imparts to the soul an imperturbable poise and a serene

---

[46] Pentecost Sequence.

calm, the character of recollectedness, the soaring lightness of a full inner freedom. He, whom the Church calls "light of the heart, sweet guest of the soul,"[47] fills us with that supernatural light which takes away the poison of enmity, dispels the gloom of depression, and dissolves the spasm of agitation. The consummate peace of the "redeemed," the peace of those whom the blood of the Lamb has reconciled to God, is borne up by the consciousness that He "in whom we live and move and are"[48] is eternal Love; that "He hath first loved us."[49] That peace is the fruit of a supernatural love for God.

For no earthly power can shatter his peace who, like the merchant in the Gospel who gave away everything he had for one costly pearl,[50] no longer seeks anything but Christ. He knows "that neither death, nor life, nor angels, nor principalities, nor powers, nor things present, nor things to come, nor might, nor height, nor depth, nor any other creature, shall be able to separate us from the love of God, which is in Christ Jesus our Lord."[51]

[47] Ibid.
[48] Acts 17:28.
[49] 1 John 4:10.
[50] Matt. 13:45-46.
[51] Rom. 8:38-39.

Making Christ's Peace a Part of Your Life

This peace is a thing immeasurably precious in itself, and most pleasing to the eyes of God; it is the special gift of the Paraclete whom Christ has promised us before His leave-taking: "My peace I give unto you."[52]

∞

Inner peace engenders outward concord

This inward peace, then, is infinitely more important even than all outward concord; however, it is not separable from the latter, but engenders it of necessity. If inward peace reigns in a man's soul — as it does in the saints' — it removes from any struggle he may have to wage the venoms of asperity and irritation, of harshness and malicious enmity. With him, the struggle for the kingdom of God becomes visibly and tangibly a struggle of peace against peacelessness.

Such a fight is always waged in the ultimate interest of the opponent, too — according to the words of St. Augustine: "To kill the error, to love the erring one."

It is a fight waged with weapons entirely different from those wielded by the adversary — with the weapons of Light. Such a struggle is inscribed with the words

[52] John 14:27.

of the Lord: "Father, forgive them, for they know not what they do."[53] For they who possess true inward peace irradiate peace even when fighting for the kingdom of God. From their being emanates an intrinsic harmony, the reflection of the infinite harmony of God; from their whole bearing and doing issues a mild and soothing light, which melts away all grimness and embitterment.

A true *soldier of Christ* is firmly entrenched in the Absolute. He conducts his actions sovereignly from an irremovable point of vantage, against which all the poisoned arrows sent by his adversaries prove powerless.

Such a style of warfare tends to disarm the antagonist and to communicate to him something of the serene calm that tints it; even to draw him irresistibly into the orbit of that victorious yet mild and redeeming light.

∞

We must also be peacemakers

But there is one more thing we must remember. The Lord says, not merely, "Blessed are they who are at peace," but, "Blessed are the *peacemakers*."[54] It does not suffice to

[53] Luke 23:34.
[54] Matt. 5:9.

love peace and to preserve it amidst inevitable conflicts; beyond that, a true Christian must also and everywhere act as a peacemaker. Wherever we witness a struggle over earthly goods or a struggle for the kingdom of God that takes the form of a mundane strife, we should be pained and grieved at the sight.

We should diligently try, in the first case, to mediate peace, and in the second, to inject the spirit of peace into the inevitable struggle for the kingdom of God and to restore that struggle to its true character. In this function of peacemakers, too, it will be most needful for us to possess true inward peace in ourselves, and that in a measure which renders it effective even by mere spontaneous *irradiation*.

All saints were peacemakers and brought peace wherever they went. A scene from St. Francis's life may provide the most touching illustration for this.

Shortly before his death, the saint was lying, gravely ill, in the episcopal palace at Assisi. "The first thing Francis learned there, after his arrival, about the affairs of his native town was that an open feud had broken out between the Podestà and the Bishop. The Bishop had pronounced an interdict against the Podestà; the latter, in his turn, had forbidden the burghers all traffic with their spiritual head. 'It should greatly shame us,' said Francis to his brethren, 'that none of us is working for peace here!' And, eager to do what was in his power, he wrote two new strophes of his *Canticle of the Sun*, and thereupon invited the Podestà to the episcopal palace where he lay bedridden, asking at the same time the Bishop to lend his presence. When the two enemies, and all others Francis had wanted to be present, were gathered in the Piazza del Vescovado (the same place where, nineteen years before, Francis had given his sumptuous robes back to his father), two friars of his brotherhood came forward and sang the *Canticle of the Sun*, first its original text, then the addition newly written by Francis:

> Praised be Thou, O Lord, for those who give
> pardon for Thy love
> and endure infirmity and tribulation;
> blessed those who endure in peace,
> who will be, Most High, crowned by Thee!

"While the two friars sang, all stood there with folded hands as when the Gospel is read in church. But when the chant was ended, with the last 'Praised be

Making Christ's Peace a Part of Your Life

Thou, O Lord' still in everybody's ears, the Podestà made a step forward, knelt down to Bishop Guido, and spoke: 'For love of our Lord Jesus Christ and His servant Francis, I forgive you from my heart and am ready to do your will, as it pleases you to bid me!'

"The Bishop then bent down, and drawing his former enemy to him, embraced and kissed him, and said: 'According to my office, it would befit me to be humble and peaceable. But of my nature I am inclined to anger; therefore thou must bear with me.' And the brethren went in and told Francis of the victory he had achieved with his song over the evil spirits of strife."[55] "Blessed are the peacemakers, for they shall be called the sons of God."[56]

In every one of us, the desire must be alive to attain inward peace, to keep peace, and to serve the peace of others. As the disciples of Him about whom St. Paul says, "Christ is your peace"[57] and whom the Church at Christmas calls *Princeps Pacis* ("Prince of Peace"), we must possess, irradiate, and spread peace. We must always stand witness to this primary word of the Gospels,

[55] Jules Jörgensen, *St. Francis of Assisi.*
[56] Matt. 5:9.
[57] Cf. Eph. 2:14.

thus giving proof that we are true disciples of Christ: "Taste and see that the Lord is sweet."[58]

In truth, he alone who has *tasted the sweetness* of the Lord can imagine what true peace is, and burn with desire for that peace. They alone can be truly transformed in Christ who say with St. Augustine: "Thou hast called me aloud, and pierced my deafness; Thou hast shone and sparkled, and chased away my blindness; Thou hast spread a sweet perfume; I have breathed it in and am longing for Thee; I have tasted, and now I hunger and thirst; Thou hast touched me, and lo! I burn with desire for Thy peace."[59]

[58] Ps. 33:9 (RSV = Ps. 34:8).
[59] *Confessions*, Bk. 10, ch. 27.

∞

Dietrich von Hildebrand
(1889-1977)

∞

Hitler feared him, and the late Pope Pius XII called him "the twentieth-century Doctor of the Church." For more than six decades, Dietrich von Hildebrand — philosopher, spiritual writer, and anti-Nazi crusader — led philosophical, religious, and political groups, lectured throughout Europe and the Americas, and published more than thirty books and many more articles. His influence was widespread and endures to this day.

Although Dietrich von Hildebrand was a deep and original thinker on subjects ranging across the spectrum of human interests, nonetheless, in his lectures and writings, he instinctively avoided extravagant speculations and convoluted theories. Instead, he sought to illuminate the nature and significance of seemingly "everyday" elements of human existence that are easily misunderstood and too frequently taken for granted. Therefore, much of von Hildebrand's philosophy concerns the human person, the person's interior ethical and affective life, and the relations that should exist between the person and the world in which he finds himself.

Von Hildebrand's background made him uniquely qualified to examine these topics. He was born in beautiful Florence in 1889, the son of the renowned German sculptor Adolf von Hildebrand. At the time, the von Hildebrand home was a center of art and culture, visited by the greatest European artists and musicians of the day. Young Dietrich's early acquaintance with these vibrant, creative people intensified his natural zest for life.

While in Florence, von Hildebrand was surrounded by beauty — the overwhelming natural beauty of the Florentine countryside and the rich beauty of the many art treasures that are Florence's Renaissance heritage. Pervading this Florentine atmosphere was Catholicism: in the art, in the architecture, and in the daily life of the people. These early years in Florence quickened in von Hildebrand a passionate love of truth, of goodness, of beauty, and of Christianity.

As he grew older, he developed a deep love for philosophy, studying under some of the greatest of the early twentieth-century German philosophers, including Edmund Husserl, Max Scheler, and Adolf Reinach. Converting to Catholicism in 1914, von Hildebrand taught philosophy for many years at the University of Munich.

However, soon after the end of World War I, Nazism began to threaten von Hildebrand's beloved southern Germany. With his characteristic clear-sightedness, von Hildebrand immediately discerned its intrinsic evil. From its earliest days, he vociferously denounced Nazism in articles and speeches throughout Germany and the rest of Europe.

Declaring himself unwilling to continue living in a country ruled by a criminal, von Hildebrand regretfully left his native Germany for Austria, where he continued teaching philosophy (now at the University of Vienna) and fought the Nazis with even greater vigor, founding and then publishing for several years a prominent anti-Nazi newspaper, *Christliche Ständestaat*.

This angered both Heinrich Himmler and Adolf Hitler, who were determined to silence von Hildebrand and close his newspaper. Orders were given to have von Hildebrand assassinated in Austria. However, he evaded the hit-squads and, thanks to his Swiss passport, was able to flee the country just as it fell to the Nazis.

It is characteristic of von Hildebrand that even while he was engaged in this life-and-death struggle against the Nazis, he maintained his deep spiritual life, and managed to write during this period his greatest work, the sublime and highly acclaimed spiritual classic *Transformation in Christ*.

Fleeing from Austria, von Hildebrand was pursued through many countries, ultimately arriving on the shores of America in 1940 by way of France, Spain, Portugal, and Brazil.

Penniless in New York after his heroic struggle against the Nazis, von Hildebrand was hired as professor of philosophy at Fordham University where he taught until his retirement. Many of his best works were written during this period and after his retirement. He died in 1977 in New Rochelle, New York.

Dietrich von Hildebrand was remarkable for his keen intellect, his profound originality, his prodigious output, his great personal courage, his deep spirituality, and his intense love of truth, goodness, and beauty. These rare qualities made him one of the greatest philosophers and one of the wisest men of the twentieth century.

∞

Sophia Institute Press®

∞

Sophia Institute is a nonprofit institution that seeks to restore man's knowledge of eternal truth, including man's knowledge of his own nature, his relation to other persons, and his relation to God.

Sophia Institute Press® serves this end in numerous ways. It publishes translations of foreign works to make them accessible for the first time to English-speaking readers, it brings back into print books that have been long out of print, and it publishes important new books that fulfill the ideals of Sophia Institute. These books afford readers a rich source of the enduring wisdom of mankind.

Sophia Institute Press® makes these high-quality books available to the public by using advanced technology and by soliciting donations to subsidize its general publishing costs.

Your generosity can help provide the public with editions of works containing the enduring wisdom of the ages. Please send your tax-deductible contribution to the address below.

For your free catalog,
call toll-free:
1-800-888-9344

or write:
Sophia Institute Press®
Box 5284
Manchester, NH 03108

or visit our website:
website: http:\\www.sophiainstitute.com

Sophia Institute is a tax-exempt institution
as defined by the Internal Revenue Code,
Section 501(c)(3). Tax I.D. 22-2548708.